THE FIRST BOOK OF
ETHICS

THE FIRST BOOK OF ETHICS

BY ALGERNON D. BLACK

DRAWINGS BY RICK SCHREITER

This book is dedicated to a great teacher who was killed in the year 399 b.c. by the people of the ancient city of Athens

Why did they kill him?
They killed him for a crime.
What was the crime?
He was accused of corrupting the young people of the city.
How did he do that
He asked questions.
Why would that hurt anybody?
By his questions he made them think.
What's wrong with that?
He made them think about things they believed.
How could that do any harm?
When people ask questions and think about things they believe, they may not believe the same after that.
And the people of Athens killed him for doing that?
Yes, they did.
Why did he do it?
Because he loved truth and he wanted to find truth.
Who was this teacher?
He was a stonecutter. He earned his living by cutting marble for the buildings and statues of the city. But in his free time he was a teacher.
What was his name?
His name was Socrates.
What subject did he teach?
His subject was ethics.

"The First Book of Ethics" by Algernon D. Black. ISBN 978-0-9897323-4-5.

Published by The American Ethical Union ©2013. All rights reserved. No part of this publication may be reproduced, stored in a retrieval system, or transmitted in any form or by any means, electronic, mechanical, recording or otherwise, without the prior written permission of The American Ethical Union.

Manufactured in the United States of America.

CONTENTS

ETHICS?	1
YOU ARE THE JUDGE	1
ETHICS IS QUESTIONS — AND ANSWERS	2
THE LAW OF THE JUNGLE	3
THE NEED FOR UNITY	3
RETALIATION: A WRONG FOR A WRONG	3
A DIFFERENT IDEA	5
A BLOOD PRICE	5
RULES FOR LIFE	5
THE MORAL CODE	6
CHANGING THE RULES	8
THE CHANGING ETHICS OF SLAVERY	9
ETHICS AND THE PHILOSOPHIES OF MAN	11
ETHICS AND THE RELIGIONS OF MAN	12
FOUR IMPORTANT COMMANDMENTS	14
YOU SHALL NOT KILL	15
YOU SHALL NOT STEAL	22
YOU SHALL NOT BEAR FALSE WITNESS	26
HONOR YOUR FATHER AND YOUR MOTHER	30
"MINUS" ETHICS, "ZERO" ETHICS, AND "PLUS" ETHICS	35
OUR FEELINGS AND OUR THOUGHTS	39
JUDGING YOURSELF	40
WHEN YOU ARE HURT	42
"GOOD" PEOPLE AND "BAD" PEOPLE	44
WHAT IS A GOOD ACT AND GOOD CONDUCT?	45
WHAT LAWS DO ABOUT ETHICS	47
CAN LAWS MAKE PEOPLE DO WHAT IS RIGHT?	51
BIG ETHICAL ISSUES	52
THREE CHALLENGES	53
HARD CHOICES	59
SOME WISE WORDS FROM THE PHILOSOPHERS	60
ETHICS IN THE STRUGGLE FOR DEMOCRACY	62
INDEX	65

ETHICS?

Ethics is the study of how people treat each other, and what it means to lead a good life.

"Is it about right and wrong?" you may ask. "Because if it is, I'm not interested. People have been telling me about right and wrong all my life. 'Do this!' and 'Don't do that!' — No more of that, thank you."

But ethics isn't what you think. With ethics, nobody is telling anybody. Ethics is questions, and a hunt for truth. Every person becomes his own judge of right and wrong.

"That sounds good," you may be thinking. "I've always wanted to be a judge and sit on a bench and decide what to do with people."

YOU ARE THE JUDGE

You are the judge, but not in the way you think. You are just like any other person. Everyone is a judge, and his court is his conscience. He must question and cross-examine himself as well as others. He must decide whether he is innocent or guilty. He may have to judge others, too. He may even have to judge the community he lives in, and the whole world.

"But what's the purpose of ethics?" you may be thinking. "What good is it?"

Ethics is a way of being a free person. It helps a person know what his choices are in life. It makes him his own judge all during

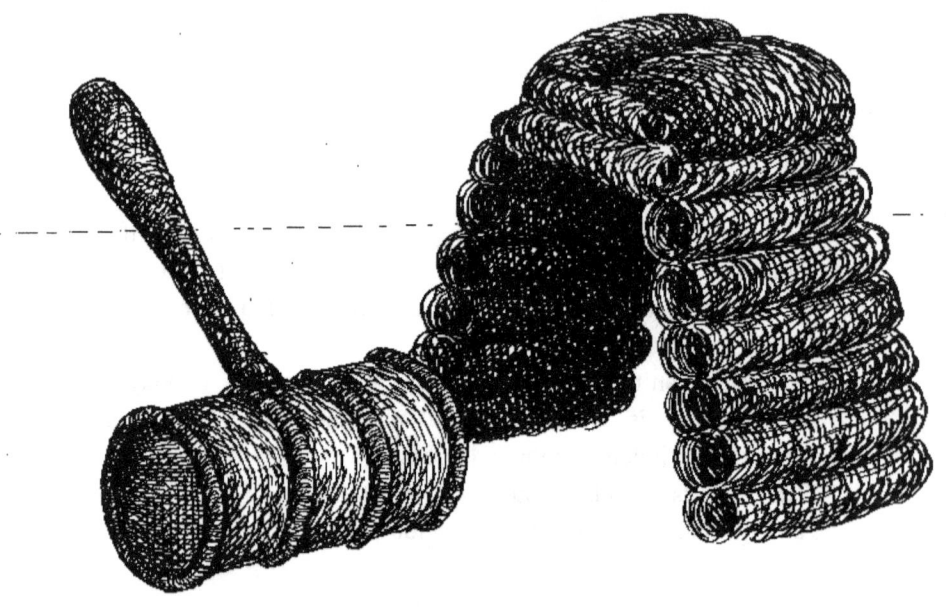

his lifetime. No matter what other people think and say and do, he is the one who decides for himself.

ETHICS IS QUESTIONS — AND ANSWERS

The questions that ethics asks are a part of the life of every person. How should people treat each other? How can we get people to be fair to each other? How can we tell what is right and what is wrong?

But how do we find the answers? To be judges, shouldn't we have some idea of justice? What is the test?

That is the big question that ethics asks: How shall we find the answers?

This book is about how people have tried to find the answers, and how each person may find them for himself.

THE LAW OF THE JUNGLE

In the jungle no animal is safe. Lions and tigers, snakes and alligators are killers. When they are hungry they hunt and kill other animals. Sometimes one animal attacks another when he feels afraid and in danger. Sometimes animals fight over food or their families. Sometimes they fight to see who will be the leader of the pack. Every animal must learn to run, or hide, or fight for its life. The strong feed on the weak, the fast on the slow, and the tricky ones on those who are witless, or careless, or asleep.

At first, the early men probably lived much like animals. They hunted and fought and killed when they needed food or had to defend themselves. There was no protection for the individual except in his own strength and skill in fighting, or in his speed in running and hiding from animals or human enemies.

THE NEED FOR UNITY

But at some point human beings in large families or in tribal communities began to see that with united strength and trust they could stand together even against a pack of dangerous wolves.

And they learned that when the members and families within a tribe were at war with one another, an enemy tribe from across the mountains could make a surprise attack and kill the men, take their wives and children as slaves, and steal all the food and weapons. But if the tribe stood together, they could defend themselves.

RETALIATION: A WRONG FOR A WRONG

In many places where people began to live in groups of families and in tribal communities it became the custom to try to pay back a wrong with a wrong. People even thought of measuring the hurt, and making a balance by doing the same amount of hurt back.

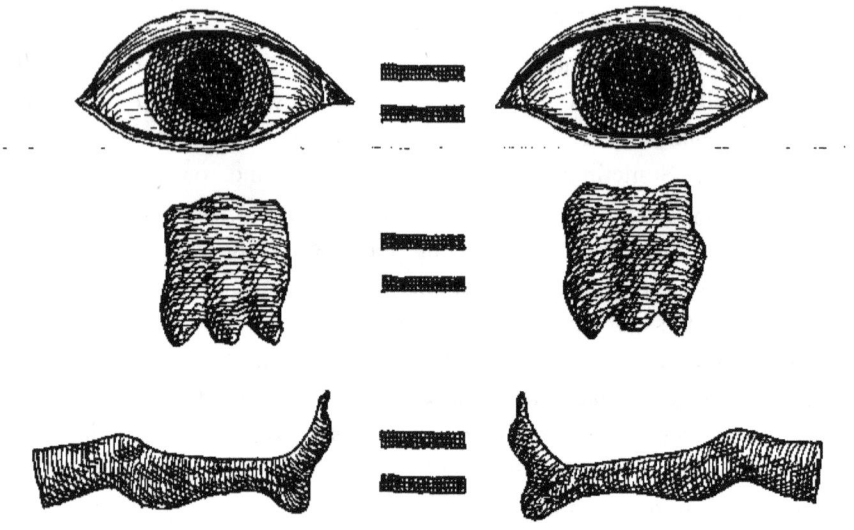

"If someone knocks out your tooth, knock out his. If someone blinds you in one eye, blind him in one eye. If someone kills your brother, kill him or his brother."

But instead of making things right, doing a wrong in return often made more wrong. If a boy pushes you, you push him. If he knocks you down, you want to knock him down. It is natural to want to "get even." But things usually turn out uneven.

When people tried to hurt those who had hurt them, they were so angry that they often did more injury than had been done them. If a man killed another man, the father or brother or son of the murdered man might be so angry that he killed more than one person. Then the other family became even more angry, and there was more fear and more hate. The fighting might go on for years and even for generations. There was no way to stop the beating and stealing and burning and killing. One wrong led to many wrongs. The only way to end the feud was for one family to kill all the members of the other family.

A DIFFERENT IDEA

Some people saw that the only hope of stopping the feuds and fighting was to get rid of the idea that "two wrongs make a right." "We can stop all this if only we don't 'do bad back,' " they thought. "Two killings don't bring the dead back to life."

A BLOOD PRICE

Someone may have said, "When an injury is done, that injury must be paid for. A man must suffer for what he has done, because if nobody retaliates he will do injury again. Then more and more people will see that they can hurt without being hurt. He or his kinsfolk, his family or his tribe, must pay for what he has done." "That makes sense," people thought. "When a hurt is done, the hurt-doer shall pay for the injury, or his family shall make a payment or a forfeit. This will even the balance. It will end the feuds and bring strength and unity to the tribe. We will put a forfeit or reparation price on a man's life, on a tooth, on an eye."

Long, long ago, some primitive tribes used this way of treating those who had done injury to others. Instead of revenge or a wrong for a wrong, and instead of blood feuds, men paid in fish or meat or furs, in weapons or tools or trinkets. Even today we hold this idea. If someone injures us, we can sue in court for payment of damages by the one who did us injury.

RULES FOR LIFE

Just as there must be rules in a game, in order to give everyone a fair chance and prevent cheating and quarrels, so there must be some regulations wherever people live together. But these guideposts for living are not exactly rules. We call them teachings or customs.

Customs are ways of behaving which are expected of everybody. Over a long period of time, people become used to them and they become a habit. The children learn them from older people and from watching the way everyone conducts himself.

In tribal communities where life is simple, it is easy for boys and girls to learn the tribal customs. They learn some things by imitating older people. Some things they are taught. They must learn how to eat and dress and speak, how to make tools and weapons, how to hunt and fish, how to gather food or grow crops or handle cattle. As soon as they are physically strong and know enough to take their parts as grown people, they are introduced into the tribe's religious beliefs and ceremonies. And they are prepared for the responsibility of marrying.

The customs and teachings usually have good reasons behind them. The clothes people wear, the food they eat, and the way they build their houses are usually due to the nature of the place where they live. Fishermen in a village by the sea are sure to have different customs from people who live by hunting, or from those who grow crops and keep cattle. How the people own and share the land — whether they live and work cooperatively, or separately and in competition — this and other arrangements may depend on the climate and whether it is easy or hard to get a living from the earth and sea. If nothing changes in the climate and if they still have water, and fishes, and animals to hunt, people may live the same way for a long, long time.

THE MORAL CODE

In every tribe and every community some customs forbid acts that violate religion and what the people believe is sacred and holy.

In every tribe and community there are also customs that regulate how people behave toward one another. These customs are part of the moral code. They are ways of family life, of marrying, of parents-and-children and brother-and-sister relationships. They are community ways of working, and owning and dividing and sharing things, and settling disputes. Because of the moral code, most people feel that they know what to expect of other people, and they know what is expected of them. Such a code helps the tribe or the community feel secure. It helps toward unity and strength.

Most people obey the moral code not because of laws and policemen, but because of habit. If they violate the code and do things that are forbidden or not approved by the community, they are punished by having people talk about them, and by being left out of many things they want to do and enjoy. They are made to feel as if they no longer belong to the community.

CHANGING THE RULES

Each tribe or community usually thinks that its own customs and teachings are the only good and true ones. The people usually assume that their customs are part of an unchangeable law of God or of nature, They think things always were this way and always will be.

If the people live off by themselves and do not have any contact with other ways of life, they may live in the same manner for centuries. But if they meet other people through trade or migration or wars, changes may occur. Whether a person lives in an Indian tribe or among the Eskimos, or whether he lives in a farm community or a big city, he is sure to get some new ideas if he travels or if someone from outside, with different customs and a different moral code, comes into his neighborhood.

A new invention or a machine can change the customs and moral code of a community. If a whole village has depended mostly on hunting or fishing and has required strong men, then the strong men might be the most respected and powerful people. But suppose a machine and a new factory make it possible for women and children and old people to earn money and support themselves and their families without depending on the strong men. Then women will begin to be more nearly equal with men. They will have more to say in running the family and governing the community. Even the marriage customs may change.

When a rifle or a radio or a jeep or modern medicine is introduced into a community, people begin to live differently and to think differently and to change their ideas of right and wrong.

The rules of life and the moral code can also change because of other things besides trade and travel and wars and new inventions. Sometimes people suffer and are so unhappy that they try to introduce new ways. Sometimes other people feel the unfairness too, and try to help make changes.

THE CHANGING ETHICS OF SLAVERY

For thousands of years in most of the world, human beings believed that it was perfectly right and good for some men to own other men. Owners acquired slaves by capturing men in battle, by kidnapping them, by buying or inheriting them, and by enslaving them in payment of debts. In the slave markets, buyers felt the slaves' legs and looked at their teeth to be sure that the person for sale would be a healthy servant or worker. Then they made bids, and the slave went to the highest bidder.

Once they owned the slaves, the masters could do what they pleased with them — work them to death, beat them, keep them in chains, starve them, or sell them. Slaves could be separated one from another even though they were man and wife or parents and children. Whether a slave had a hard or an easy life depended on only one thing: the kindness or cruelty of his master. The slave had no rights and no protectors.

Nobody seemed to question this custom. Most people believed that slavery was God's law. Even such great thinkers as the Greeks Plato and Aristotle thought that some men were born to be slaves and others were born to be masters. Athens, the great center of Greek culture which prided itself on being a democracy, had slaves. The Romans also believed in slavery. Just as the ancient Egyptians used slaves to construct their great pyramids and palaces, so the Romans used them to build roads and aqueducts and the great Colosseum. The Romans also used slaves as gladiators to entertain the masses of people in the Circus Maximus and the Colosseum.

But even though slavery was accepted in the ancient world, there were some individuals who felt it was wrong. In some places, slaves tried to run away or buy their freedom. Some organized revolts.

As the centuries passed, slavery made more and more people uncomfortable in their consciences. Some religious people such as the Quakers freed their own slaves. Some people raised their voices

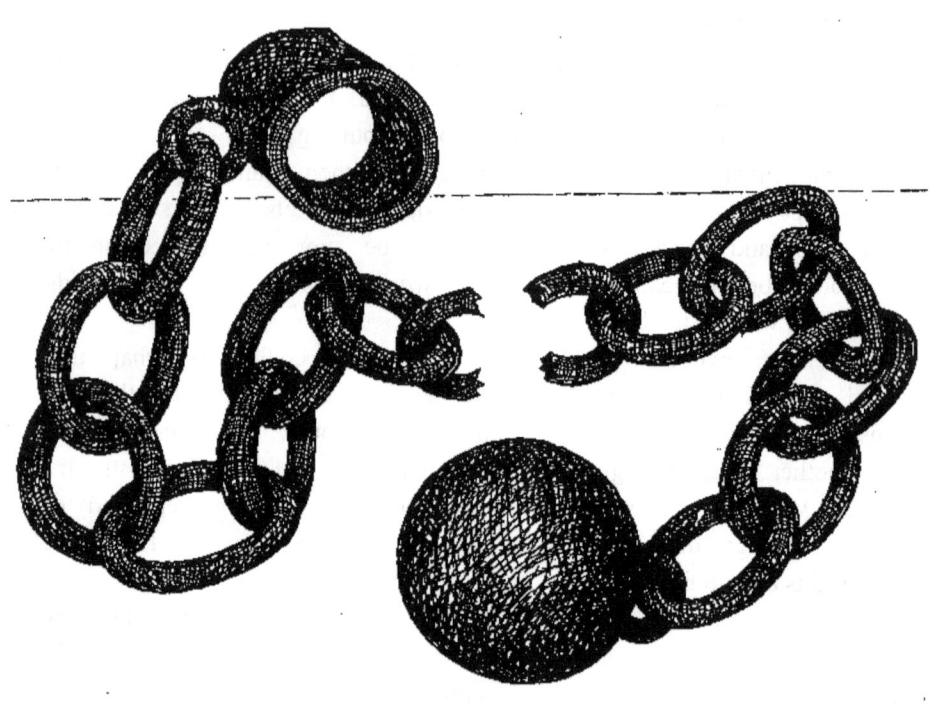

for the abolition of slavery. In Europe, the nations had outlawed slavery by 1850. In the United States, men who had strong passions against slavery preached, printed newspapers and books, and became Abolitionists — people who wished to do away with slavery. To them, slavery was unethical even if the slave owners were kind. The Abolitionists were determined to change the customs and the code under which slavery was accepted by the community. One of their leaders, Elijah Lovejoy, was killed because he spoke and printed arguments against slavery. John Brown was hanged for daring to try to help the slaves by giving them arms so that they could fight for their freedom. It took a bitter and bloody Civil War to rid the United States of the idea that some men could own other men.

The movement to abolish slavery is an example of the criticism and changing of a moral code. Although at one time almost everybody everywhere accepted slavery as a moral custom, more and more people began to feel and think that it was wrong. They dared to judge the moral custom of their society and to make sacrifices for their ethical beliefs. This is the way progress comes — the way the conscience of mankind grows and broadens and deepens.

ETHICS AND THE PHILOSOPHIES OF MAN

The word "ethics" comes from the Greek word *ethos,* meaning "character" or "custom." The ancient Greeks thought a great deal about life and death. Because they traveled and traded and fought with many different peoples, they came to know that there were many different ways of living and believing. The Greeks began to ask: What is man? What is man's relation to nature? What is a good life? What is justice?

Those who asked these questions, and thought, and tried to supply the answers, became known as teachers and philosophers. Philosophy means "love of wisdom." The Greek "lovers of wisdom" held discussions and wrote out their ideas of what they meant by a good life. Because this happened among the Greek people at least 2,300 years ago, we say that the interest in ethics came from the Greek philosophers. But philosophers in every civilization — in the ancient Roman and ancient Chinese and Hindu, and in modern European and American civilizations — have all asked questions and given us wise answers in matters of ethics.

ETHICS AND THE RELIGIONS OF MAN

Every religion has had teachers and holy men and prophets who have tried to help people understand what is right and wrong and what is good and evil. In the bibles of the great religions of the world are many teachings and commandments which are part of the ethical heritage of mankind.

Even though the various world religions grew up at different times, and in different parts of the world, and in countries with differing languages and customs and civilizations, they have all tended to arrive at the same place in their ideas about ethics. They have all arrived at the belief that every human being is sacred and holy, that every person should be respected as having value in himself, that there is something in every person that should not be destroyed or violated.

A second belief growing out of this one is that people should respect and be fair to one another.

From Egyptian Religion

The people who lived in the Nile Valley five thousand years ago believed that at death every person's soul would have to appear in the Hall of Truth, where forty-two judges would decide what was to happen to the soul in another world. There the soul was judged according to the way the person had lived. Three questions among the many that were asked are still important:

Hast thou taken the life of thy brother?
Hast thou been guilty of theft?
Has thy tongue spoken falsely against thy neighbor?

From Babylonian Religion

The people who lived in the land between the Tigris and Euphrates rivers four thousand years ago also had developed ideas of how people should deal with each other. From all parts of the empire the ruler Hammurabi gathered the ideas of right and wrong and had them cut in the black stone wall near the great temple in Babylon.

From Judaism

Moses brought the Ten Commandments down from Mount Sinai for the guidance of the tribes of Israel. These commandments were based not on the belief in many gods, but on the belief in one God. And three of the commandments were the same as those which were taught by the Egyptians and the Babylonians::

Thou shalt not kill.
Thou shalt not steal.
Thou shalt not bear false witness.

There were more than 613 commandments which judges and teachers and prophets taught the people. Many of them were "Thou shalt not" commandments, too. For example:

Thou shalt not put a stumbling block in the path of the blind.

Thou shalt not take a man's tools or his millstones in payment for debt.

And the first general rule that was taught was, *Do not do unto others that .which you would not want others to do unto you.*

From Christianity

Jesus said, "You have heard it said, 'Thou shalt love thy neighbor and hate thine enemy,' but I say unto you, Love your enemies, bless them that curse you, do good to them that hate you.

"You have heard it said, 'An eye for an eye and a tooth for a tooth,' but I say unto you, Resist not evil, but if anyone strike you on your right cheek, then turn to him the other also."

The idea of the brotherhood of all human beings is common to all great faiths.

FOUR IMPORTANT COMMANDMENTS

Among the teachings of the great philosophies and religions, past and present, four commandments are common to all. They are as timely today as they were when men first thought of them and made them part of the moral custom and the rules to live by. Three are "You shall not" commandments, and one is a "You shall" commandment. They are these:

You shall not kill.

You shall not steal.

You shall not bear false witness.

You shall honor your father and your mother.

YOU SHALL NOT KILL

Animals kill without feelings. When they are hungry they track and trap their prey. When they are in danger they fight their enemies to the death. When a lion kills a deer, or a hawk kills a chicken, he has no feelings except the satisfaction of getting what he wants and the pleasure of eating it. He feels no shame or guilt or pity. It is as natural for him to kill as for rain to fall from the sky or for water to flow downstream to the sea.

Some people say that men developed customs and rules against killing because they had to if they wanted to survive.

We don't know all the reasons, but there came a time when men began to feel that it was wrong to kill.

For example, a man killed another man in a fight. After it was over, he couldn't forget the face of the man he had killed. He remembered the grieving of the man's wife and children. He felt ashamed that he had done this wrong to a man smaller and weaker than himself. He was afraid to go near the place where the man had lived, and the place of the killing. He wished that he himself could be forgiven and the man could come back to life. He wished he could wash his hands and feel that they did not have blood on them.

We do not know when human beings first began to have these feelings against the taking of human life. We do know that people felt this way at least five thousand years ago. At that time they wrote some of their ideas on papyrus and cut them into clay tablets and in stone.

In the Book of the Dead, the Egyptians wrote that at the judging of the soul the person questioned had to be able to swear that he had *not* done certain things: "I have not brought misery on my fellows. I have not caused hunger or weeping. I have not slain or given orders to slay."

We human beings have outgrown some of the very old ways. We no longer kill other human beings to eat them, as cannibals did. We no longer kill human beings as a sacrifice to the gods. We no longer kill people as witches and sorcerers. We no longer kill people for minor offenses.

But we still kill far too many people. Many deaths are due to personal jealousy, hate, and greed. Many are due to carelessness and accidents that could be avoided. Too many people break speed and traffic laws on the highways. Too many people live in unsafe buildings and work in factories where there is poor protection from the machinery. Far too many human beings suffer from sickness that they could escape if they could work and buy the food and other things they need. And far too many human beings are killed in wars all over the world.

The Hidden Assumption

The teaching, "You shall not kill," is based on the assumption that every human life has something that makes it of special value. There are many reasons, religious and ethical, for this assumption. But the thing all can agree about is that every person has only one life — only one chance to live and fulfill himself. And every individual is different. No one else has the same combination of looks, and ways of feeling and thinking and doing. Every individual is unique. Nobody can ever be duplicated or replaced. For these reasons every life is priceless. To kill a person is to destroy the most precious and sacred thing we know.

Most people have no desire or impulse to kill. For them it is not a matter of fear or punishment. They have a sense of the sacredness of life, and they love life for themselves and for other people.

But some who have a strong feeling against taking human life think that sometimes killing may be justified.

Is Killing Ever Justified? What About Self-Defense?

Most people think that if your life is threatened you are justified in defending yourself and fighting and even killing the person who tries to destroy you. Is it right to assume that the person who has no respect for human life and who wants to kill you is less worthy to live than you, who have no desire to kill anyone and who have a respect for life?

What About Defending Someone Else?

Do you think you are justified in killing a person if you act in defense of someone else who cannot defend himself, such as a child or a very old person or possibly a woman attacked by a man, or an unarmed person attacked by an armed person?

Do you think you are not justified unless you have used every

other method and have tried to stop the killer, or incapacitate him, first?

Suppose a policeman sees that a man is shooting at people in the street. The man will not listen to anyone. He has already wounded or killed at least one person. Everyone is in danger. Is it right for the policeman to shoot at the man and take his life for the sake of others? Suppose he calls on the man to stop. Suppose he tries to shoot him in the leg or arm to stop him without killing him. Suppose he kills him. Should the policeman be excused for doing this? Should he be praised for doing it? Is it his duty?

Suppose the person who is doing wrong is not killing, but is robbing a person by holding him up, or is robbing a home or a bank. Can killing a robber be justified? In such a case, does it make a difference whether the robber was taking a few dollars from a person, or some goods from a store, or a large sum from a bank? What if he is stealing a secret necessary to the safety of the country?

Some people say, "I will never kill under any circumstances — even if I am being killed. Killing is always wrong. It never makes right. It solves no problems. It only leads to more killing. Do not try to force me to kill, even for a good purpose. We cannot serve a good purpose by bad means."

Nonviolent Resistance to Evil

Jesus believed that "You shall not kill" applied to all human situations. He would not defend himself or further a good cause by violent means. Others have used the teaching and method of nonviolence to try to prevent strife and win respect for basic rights.

Mahatma Gandhi, who used nonviolent means to help win India's independence from Great Britain, said that the highest duty of a citizen was to oppose evil by nonviolent means. "Violence begets violence," he said. "Nonviolence is the greatest force at the disposal of mankind."

Capital Punishment

Is it right for the community to practice capital punishment — to execute a person for committing a crime? What can justify a community for deliberately taking the life of an individual? Should human beings ever decide whether or not another human being is fit to live?

—Capital punishment used to be the penalty for hundreds of offenses. Now it is used for only a few crimes such as murder and kidnapping. But more and more people believe it should be abolished completely. In some states and countries this has been done.

People who are against capital punishment argue like this: Capital punishment may mean the killing of an innocent man. When this happens, there is no way of ever correcting the mistake. Or the person who committed the crime may be mentally sick. To deal with him as if he were an evil person is a violation of the human conscience. Punishment seldom stops people from doing wrong, and it seldom changes or improves people. On the contrary, to kill a person makes it impossible for him to change or improve. Punishment, especially capital punishment, is a way for people to hurt someone instead of facing their own responsibilities as citizens. The way to get rid of crime is to study the causes and to reeducate the wrongdoer. Punishment deals with effects, not causes, of wrongdoing. Get rid of poverty and slums. Try to make good families and homes and better schools. Try to arrange better opportunities for all people to work and earn money so that they can be productive and enjoy life.

Those who favor capital punishment argue like this: If it is abolished, we shall have more crime and more murders. Some people are regular killers; they kill people they don't like and they kill for money; some of them even kill without any reason at all. People who have no respect for life are dangerous and should not be allowed to live in the community. Such people are incurable. It is no kindness to keep them locked up all their lives. Death is better.

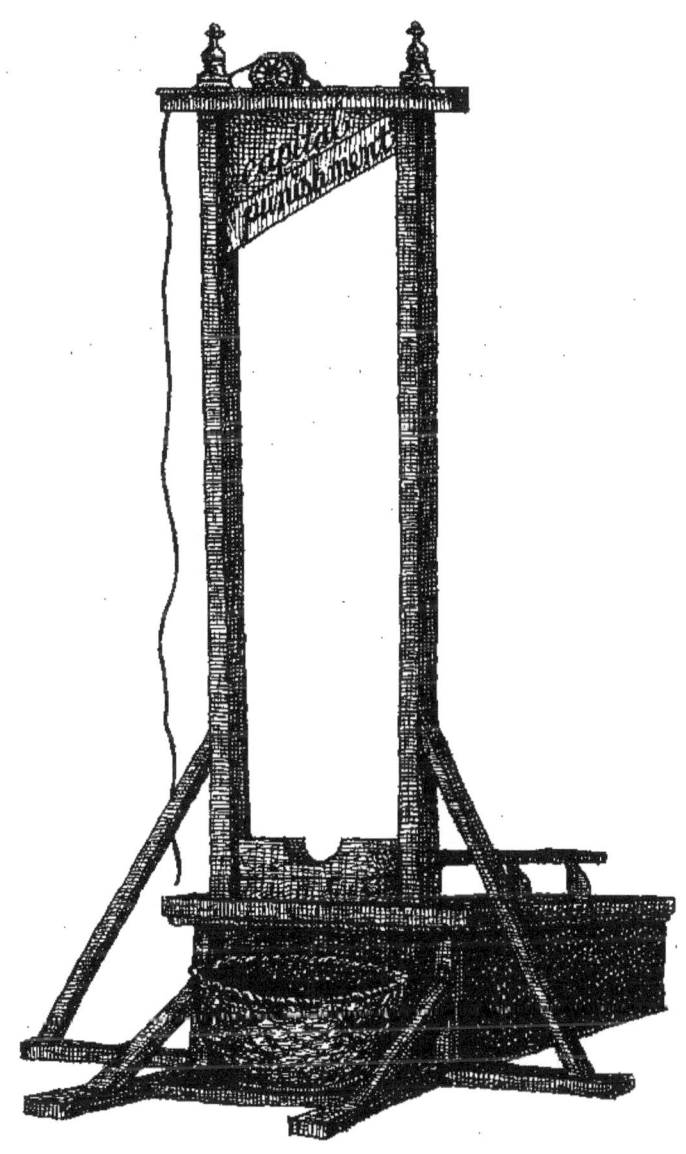

YOU SHALL NOT STEAL

Stealing means taking someone else's property without his permission or without paying him for it. The property may be taken from the owner by force or in his absence or while he is asleep. It may be taken by cheating or trickery.

When we were very young we had no idea that anybody owned anything. We grabbed whatever we could reach. Later we learned that some things were ours and some things belonged to other people.

One way to make us happy was to give us something. One way to make us unhappy was to take something away. We learned that there was pleasure in touching and playing with things and in owning things. To feel that a shoe or a comb or a toy was ours; to be given a present such as a pen or a watch or a radio — this gave us joy.

How Important Are Things?

Everyone needs certain things for living: food, clothing, shelter —a place to sleep and be safe. Most people want enough extra food so that they do not have to live from one meal to the next. They want enough things to make life a little more safe and comfortable. Without some margin above what they need at the moment, people cannot be really free.

Things are not important in themselves, but only when they serve important values or purposes. A person might take your camera or your radio, and this might upset you. But it would not endanger your life or even lessen your comfort. But if someone takes your food when you are starving and there is no other food; if someone takes your water when you are dying of thirst; if someone takes your sweater or coat or fur in the midst of a bitter winter storm, the theft can mean your death. If someone takes your work tools, you may not be able to work or care for your family.

Hurting by Taking

Some things hold special value to us personally. The picture of someone we love, or letters written especially to us, cannot be replaced. They have a value beyond any price. And there are things which we made ourselves, or which we were given, or bought at a special time, and which have special meaning because of the personal memory. If someone took these, we would be very upset.

If the person who took our possessions used force or cheated us or tricked us or borrowed things without any intention of returning them, this would hurt us even more. And if the person who took our things was a friend whom we trusted, this would make the hurt worst of all.

When we take something that belongs to someone else, we may be troubled and unhappy afterward. We may be afraid that someone will find us out and that we will be punished. Even if it is not a serious theft, we may be ashamed to have people know that we did it. Or we may feel guilty, and wish that we hadn't stolen and that there were some way we could return what we took and get rid of the feeling of guilt. For even if we are never caught or found out, we cannot enjoy the thing we have taken. We shall always remember that it is not really ours. And it will remind us that we are not as honest as we would like to be.

We may even be helped if we are caught. For then we may learn a lesson and not steal again.

From the time of the earliest records it is evident that people have seen that stealing makes for fear and hatred. It makes for fighting and killing and retaliation. It divides and weakens a people. It is harmful to those who work and lose what they produce. It is harmful to those who take things. People who live by taking things from others or from the public rarely produce anything, and usually they fail to develop their own talents. They become parasites. When someone stronger and more able comes along, he takes whatever they have. There is no security or justice in the doctrine, "Might makes right," or "Take whatever you can."

For these reasons, human beings recognized a long time ago that customs and teachings and rules must help people keep what they had found or made or bought or had been given by others.

There Are Many Ways of Stealing

There are many ways of stealing besides actually holding somebody up or breaking into a house and robbing it. Here are some ways that are not so obvious:

Charging high and excessive interest to people who need to borrow money.

Watering meat so that it weighs more, and watering milk.

Cheating on weights and measures so that people get less than they think they get.

Cutting down on the size of portions in restaurants and on the size of packages of cereal, tobacco, chocolate bars, and other things.

Overcharging.

Giving back too little change.

Getting a monopoly on something people need and then charging more than the price would be if there were fair competition.

Underpaying workers, and overworking workers.

Moving boundary marks.

Charging for repairs that are never made.

Robbing people of their time by keeping them waiting.

Robbing people of what they pay for in theater and concert by disturbing them so that they do not enjoy the performance.

Robbing students of education by disturbing the class and making it impossible for the teacher to teach and the students to learn.

Is Stealing Always Wrong?

But is stealing never justified? What if a man's family is starving? Must he not steal food if there is no other way to get it? What if a man's parents are sick and suffering and there is no way of buying or borrowing or being given medicine? Is he not justified in taking it? If a man steals for himself, it is not the same as when he steals for others. When a man steals to have something he wants, or to sell to become rich, that is different from taking bread when he or his family is starving. Do you agree or disagree? To steal is wrong. Yes, but -

Is it worse for a person to steal bread for his hungry family than for a man to hoard and keep much more than he needs, when he knows that others are hungry? Do we not make a hero of Robin Hood, who stole from the rich and gave to the poor?

YOU SHALL NOT BEAR FALSE WITNESS

At some time, when someone has called us names, we all may have said, "Sticks and stones can break my bones, but words can never hurt me," Is it true?

Words can hurt if someone gossips and spreads false rumors about what we have done. Whether we admit it or not, we do care what people think and say about us. A person's respect for himself, his chance to enjoy life, to find work and get married and enjoy good relations with his neighbors depend on his good name and reputation.

A man's reputation may be as important to him as his life. A doctor cannot practice or have patients, or work in a good hospital, unless people believe that he is a good physician and that he can be trusted. So it is with a lawyer, a teacher, a scientist, and a minister. Without a good name a man may lose his friends. He may lose his job. He may be unable to rent an apartment or buy a house. He cannot borrow money at the bank. And he cannot hold a government job or be elected to public office. So rumors or lies spread by jealous or prejudiced persons can do great damage.

If there is one thing we can all agree about it is that no (5fie should be blamed or punished for something he did not do. And it is surely dishonest and unfair to say that someone did a wrong that he did not do. It is even worse if you or I try to make people believe that someone else did a wrong which we ourselves did. If a word from anyone's lips can cause a person to be condemned by

his neighbors or punished by the courts for something he did not do, then that word is evil and the one who spoke it has done evil.

Sometimes a person can also do wrong by refusing to say what he knows. He may be quiet because he is afraid. He may be silent because he wants to protect his friends or his gang. He may not want to take the time from his own affairs to speak the truth, or he may .not want to get involved. Much evil has been hidden and many injustices have been done because people kept silence and concealed the truth.

Secrets and Privacy

On the other hand, words can sometimes hurt and do harm when someone tells things which we feel are personal and private. We know that persons such as doctors, lawyers, and ministers of religion are bound by their professions to keep confidential anything we tell them and anything they learn about us. Teachers and members of our families are also supposed to keep secret the information we may give them in private.

Our parents are not supposed to tell other people what we do, especially our mistakes or the things which we feel are our own business. Our friends are supposed to keep the secrets we tell them, just as we are supposed to keep their secrets.

Words can sometimes hurt, even if they are true. We are hurt when someone tattles on us. When a brother or a sister or a friend or a classmate tells other people something we have done, we may be blamed or punished and we may feel we can no longer trust that person.

Name-Calling

Words can hurt, too, when they make us feel that we are not as good as other people or that we do not belong or that we are no good at all. The worst hurt anyone can do is to rob us of our confidence and our respect for ourselves.

Words can hurt when they carry a false impression of a particular family or church or school or race or nationality. Words can make false pictures of people so that we may never try to find out the good in those people or learn the truth about them.

Words can carry contempt and hate and make people afraid and angry. Words can make people want to hurt, and even fight and kill each other.

White Lies

There may be times when it is better not to speak the entire truth. To tell a person he is ugly, or not intelligent, or a poor athlete may not be a kindness or even helpful. To be silent rather than speak a harmful truth may be generous and fair. To give a compliment to encourage a person and make him feel better about himself may be a good thing, even when it is not entirely deserved. For words can be friendly and can lift people's spirits.

False and True Promises

Words can hurt when they are promises on which we rely, but which fool and betray us. For many people, the most important thing in life is to be able to depend on other people. When a person does not keep his promise, he might be forgiven the first time. But what if he forgets many times?

If a friend lends you money and you promise to return it before evening, do you consider that you have a duty and an obligation to keep your word?

Suppose a person has no intention of keeping his promise even at the time he makes it. Let us say he borrows a book or some money, and he knows that he is going away and won't ever be able to give it back.

Suppose a person just won't take the time or make the effort, or always leaves it to the last moment, to get the book back or the money returned.

Suppose a person intended to return the money and would have done so, but he became sick or was hurt in an accident.

What would you think?

HONOR YOUR FATHER AND YOUR MOTHER

This is not a "You shall not" commandment. This is positive. But what does it mean to "honor" your father and your mother? Does it mean respect? Obey? Like? Love? Take care of?

It means all these things. They are easy to do, and a pleasure, when a person has parents who are dependable and generous and loving to him, and big-hearted to other people. It is easy to respect and obey human beings who are intelligent and beautiful and honorable.

You might say that no one should be asked to respect parents who are dishonorable. It is hard for sons and daughters to honor parents who are weak, or mean and narrow and crooked, or who steal; or break the law. How can a son or daughter really respect them?

Nobody is perfect. Parents often have their own problems and sicknesses and unhappiness, just as their children do. Take the story of Noah in the Old Testament. Noah was considered such a good man that he was saved when everyone else was punished in the

Flood. Well, one day Noah drank too much wine. Maybe he had trouble; maybe his cows took sick or his sheep were lost, or maybe someone cheated him in the marketplace. Suppose his wife nagged him, or one of his sons was arrested for juvenile delinquency. Anyway, he drank too much. Now when he lay there drunk and smelling of wine and snoring, some of his sons laughed, and made fun of him. But two of his sons respected him. They carried him inside the tent and covered him.

Sometimes parents' trouble is temporary. Sometimes it lasts all through their lives. And if their marriage is not completely happy, they may have difficulty in working it out. They may be trying to do so in order to keep the family together for the sake of their sons and daughters.

If you have feelings of resentment or criticism, it may be that you feel strongly just because you want so much to trust and admire and love your father and mother. This feeling of need is strong even in those who hate their parents. Deeper than the feelings of hate is the sense of family and loyalty.

Just as parents will stand by their sons and daughters even when they have been difficult and disobedient, and even when they are in serious trouble, so it is reasonable to ask that sons and daughters stand by their parents when they are old or ill or in trouble.

But what of the son or daughter who says, "Why should I bother about my parents? I don't owe them a thing. I didn't ask to be born. I didn't ask them to take care of me. At times they were pretty rough, too, with their 'Don't do this' and 'Don't do that' and their punishments. I'm grown up now, and on my own. I don't need them. If they are old and sick, it's just too bad."

A Relationship That Lasts

There is something about the human family that is very important. Often after animals mate or when their young are ready to

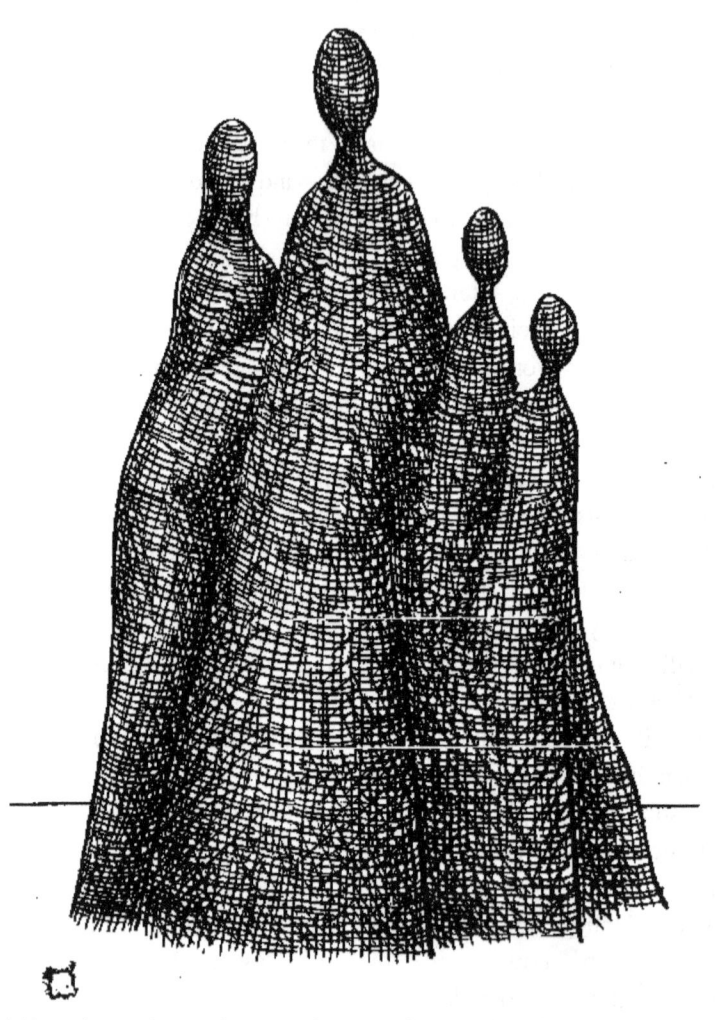

shift for themselves, the male and female separate. Their relationship is only a temporary one. But when a man and woman mate, they establish a family and a home. The relationship of the parents to each other and to their children lasts all through life. The most tender feelings of trust and love begin in the relationship of a child to his mother, and later to his father. A person's feelings, those of unhappiness as well as happiness, come from his earliest experiences in his family and his home. Because of this, the family is a very important institution of society.

And because the life of every tribe and nation and the entire human race depends on the birth and, as importantly, on the rearing of children, the commandment to honor parents is a special and positive teaching. If the sons and daughters respect their parents, it is a sign that the parents are worthy of respect and that the children are well brought up. If the sons and daughters do not respect or obey or care for their parents, it is a sign that the parents are either at fault as human beings or they have done a poor job as parents. In that case, the whole community is in trouble, for someday it will have to depend on the kind of people the sons and daughters are.

Obedience

Why have almost all human communities insisted that the children should obey? It is easy to imagine that when a tribe was in danger, as in a forest fire or earthquake or enemy attack, it had to make the children do things whether they wanted to or not. Otherwise, the children might be killed or they might endanger the whole tribe. Today, in time of family difficulty and danger, the parents and other older people have to take command. They cannot permit disobedience. They have no time to argue or explain.

When we are very young we learn that we are expected to do as we are told. If we obey we get a smile and a pat on the head, and maybe a cookie. If we disobey we get dark and angry looks, and maybe a punishment.

We obey our parents because we depend on them and need them. We want them to be kind and good to us. We obey them because they are bigger and stronger than we are. We obey them because we know that they care about us, and we trust them to know what is best for us. We trust them to know about life and to know us and to be wise. We obey them because we love them.

By doing what they want, we begin to learn their ways and their ideas. By watching them and imitating them, we learn their opinions on how to behave and what they think is right and wrong.

But as we grow older we have trouble about obeying them. *First,* there are things we want to do, and they say, "No!" *Second,* we see that other boys and girls are permitted by their parents to do the very same things. *Third,* we really want to grow up and be free to decide and learn things for ourselves. *Fourth,* there comes a time when we care about having friends and being popular with the boys and girls our own age. We find that their ideas are different from our parents' ideas.

When this happens, we have a problem. It may be serious. We want to be happy at home, but we also want to be part of the gang. When our parents and the gang press us to do opposite things, whom shall we listen to? How shall we decide? Boys and girls often complain that they are treated like children. "You forget how much I have grown up," and "You still treat me as if I were a two-year-old." These are common arguments to parents.

"Well, grow up, then," says Father. "Stop being a child and let's see you behave like a grown-up."

If our parents were always near to tell us what to do and if we always obeyed them, we would never grow up. We would never be able to decide what kind of persons we wanted to be. We have to learn for ourselves what we mean by a good life and we have to make more and more of our own decisions and choices. It is the only way to become free and responsible human beings. Our parents know this. That is why, even when we are little, they try to help us develop a conscience of our own.

"MINUS" ETHICS, "ZERO" ETHICS, AND "PLUS" ETHICS

"Minus" Ethics

Most of the commandments and teachings are "You shall nots." Three very important "You shall not" commandments have been discussed.

Nobody likes always to be told, "Don't do this!" or "Don't do that!"

What is the largest part of a policeman's job? Isn't it to prevent people from hurting each other, rather than to get them to help each other? If a policeman can stop people from breaking the law, he is doing his job. He might like to help people more often.

Maybe it's the same with other people who carry responsibility. Tribal chiefs and kings like Hammurabi, and leaders like Moses, thought that if only they could stop people from killing, stealing, and bearing false witness, everybody would be safer, and the community and the nation would be stronger and happier.

Don't — the Many Ways of Hurting

Man killing man.
Man torturing, maiming, and crippling man.
Man enslaving man.
Man taking advantage of man.
Man robbing man.

Man cheating, tricking, asking excessive interest, using false weights and measures, drawing false boundaries, moving boundary markers, adulterating goods.

Man damaging his neighbor's land, flooding fields, polluting streams, setting fire to trees, obstructing streams, letting animals loose.

Man bearing false witness, slandering, and libeling man.

Man breaking promises and contracts with man.

Man betraying man.

Man rejecting and excluding man.

Man beating down another human being's self-respect and self-confidence and desire to live.

"Zero" Ethics.

Some people take a kind of neutral approach. It's neither one way or the other. Their definition of "good" is "not doing bad."

Some people say, "I don't want to hurt anybody. Isn't that enough of a definition of being good?"

The question is, Is it possible? And if it were possible to live without hurting, what would you think of the definition?

A woman is attacked and robbed. Ten people stand watching across the street. "I didn't do anything. I don't want to get involved. I mind my own business," they might say. "That is the right way to live."

At the end of a person's life the epitaph on his tombstone might read:

He never did anything wrong. He never killed anyone or robbed or cheated anyone. He never broke the laws.
He never was arrested or imprisoned. He didn't have a police record. He never said anything bad. He had no enemies.

But did he ever do anything good?

"Plus" Ethics

Even the ancient Egyptians knew that it wasn't enough for a person to say that he hadn't done evil. Over four thousand years ago they thought that a person should be able to say that he had done some good.

I have given bread to the hungry and drink to those who have thirst. I have clothed the naked. I have healed the sick and have comforted those who mourn.

Among the 613 commandments of the Torah, or Law of Righteousness of the tribes of Israel, were some positive commandments and teachings.

Thou shalt leave the corners of the fields for the poor.

Thou shalt care for the fatherless and the widow and the poor and the aged and the stranger at the gate.

In the Old Testament it is recorded in Isaiah, *Seek justice, relieve the oppressed, judge the fatherless, plead for the widow.*

In the New Testament it is written that Jesus taught the commandments and said, *"Thou shalt love thy neighbor as thyself."*

The Golden Rule

Although some statements of the Golden Rule by various teachers and prophets were in the negative — *Do not do unto others that which thou wouldst not have others do unto you* — most of the teachers of the great religions and philosophies agree on a positive idea: *Do unto others that which thou wouldst have others do unto you.*

The real question is, What would you want others to do unto you? You might say that you don't want anyone to hurt you or wrong you. Or you might want more than this. You. might want others to help you live. You might want other human beings to help you in the following ways, and you might be willing and ready to help them, too.

Do — the Many Ways of Helping

Man protecting, defending, and rescuing man.

Man feeding, clothing, and sheltering man.

Man healing, curing, and preventing sickness in man.

Man teaching and liberating man.

Man welcoming, including, and tolerating man.

Man appreciating man.

Man encouraging and opening new doors to man.

Man understanding, trusting, and communicating with man.
Man competing and cooperating with man.
Man sharing power with man.
Man exchanging resources with man.
Man challenging, stimulating, and enhancing man.
Man showing compassion and love for man.

OUR FEELINGS AND OUR THOUGHTS

Should you feel guilty if you are jealous of someone? Should you feel afraid, and ashamed of being afraid, when you have to go into a dangerous place or among people who might seem strange or might hurt you? Should you feel ashamed if you have sexual feelings and physical desires?

All these feelings are natural and human. There is nothing evil about them. The real question is what you do about them. If you let them lead you to do things that hurt you or hurt other people, then they can be bad. But most boys and girls have such feelings and manage to understand that they are a part of being a human being and a part of growing up.

You can't take everything you want. You can't be star in the play or captain of the team or President of the United States just because you might want to be. And you can't kiss everybody who attracts you, either.

There is nothing wrong in having feelings and thinking thoughts if you make them serve your true benefit. You can work harder for the things you want. You can study and learn and grow to be such a person that you can make the team or get a part in the play or serve on the council — or something else that will prove to you that you can do things worth doing. And if you grow the right way you can attract people to like you and love you and want you. Then you can have wonderful friendships with people of your own sex and of the other sex, too. This is the road to real love and marriage and a happy life.

JUDGING YOURSELF

How you feel about yourself is very important. You must feel that you are good for something and that you have a value in yourself and for other people. This does not mean that you have to be good in a narrow way — always doing what you are told is right, never making mistakes. A person can feel good about himself even if he does so-called bad things. A person may feel bad about himself even if he does good things. If a person does bad things but really does not mean any harm to anyone, if he forgets or is mischievous, how can anyone say he is a really bad person? If a person always obeys his parents and teachers, always minds the rules, never even thinks for himself, always does what he is told, can we say that he is really good?

We all make mistakes. Sometimes we don't think about what we are doing. Sometimes it seems that our feelings control us rather

than that we control them. Sometimes we are under pressure from outside, too. We are behind in schoolwork and are afraid to fail or get a poor grade and upset our parents. So we cheat. Or because we are jealous we act mean. Or we are afraid and we run. But whatever we do, we have to face it honestly and forgive ourselves and try again.

It is what is inside a person's mind and heart that matters. When boys and girls are growing up they sometimes have to learn through their mistakes. They should not be judged just by their errors. Some of the finest men and women in the world did wrong things and played mischievous tricks when they were young. They learned. They grew up.

WHEN YOU ARE HURT

You can't live without being hurt in some way by somebody sometime. The question is, Are you hurt by accident or on purpose? Are you hurt in your body or are you hurt in your feelings and thoughts?

The worst hurt is not one to your body. The worst hurt is one that makes you feel that you can't do things or that you are ugly or that you are good for nothing — that you are *worth less* or *worthless.* That is so because in order to live and do anything and have any fun out of life you must believe in yourself and you must like yourself.

First, you must have such a belief in yourself and such a feeling about your own worth that nobody can hurt you by saying untrue things to you or about you, by taking things from you, by being unfair, by closing doors in your face and shutting you out of a game or club. You must be so strong that these things don't really make you feel less sure of yourself. You have to be strong. Trust yourself!

Second, when you judge a person, you should remember the teaching, "Judge not, that ye be not judged." Remember not to judge harshly, as if you were perfect and had never done anything wrong yourself. You should judge a person only after getting to know a great deal about him, and learning the facts. Where there is knowledge there can be understanding. To understand is to forgive. To forgive means that you bear no grudge, that you do not hate, that you do not want revenge. To forgive does not mean that you ignore the hurt done to you or that you have to like or love the person who did the hurt. The important thing is not to be so hurt by what he did that you grow mean and twisted, and have to hurt others because you were hurt.

When you are hurt you can become stronger in two ways. *First,* you can know your own worth and be more healthy and more of a person than ever before. *Second,* you can rise above hurt and go

42

beyond your own small and angry feelings to a larger and deeper understanding of other people, of the very ones who tried to hurt you.

"GOOD" PEOPLE AND "BAD" PEOPLE

The more we learn about ourselves and why we behave the way we do, the more we hesitate to put a label on somebody and say, "This person is good," and "This person is bad." It is not always easy to know what is right. It is not always easy to do what is right. Some people have more opportunity than others. Some have a harder life than others. And some are denied any chance at all to learn what it means to be fair or to do what is right or to know how to be happy alone and with other people. Some people have the good fortune to make only little mistakes, and they learn in time to correct themselves. Some make big mistakes, and do not have a chance to learn. When men or women end up in prison for serious crimes they have done against other people and against the community, it is a tragedy for everybody. Whether they kill or hurt people, whether they steal or set fire to property, whether they terrorize people — whatever hurt they do — it is because they never learned. Maybe this is because they were never taught and never had an opportunity to know the wise ways of living or the difference between right and wrong.

Even the worst person has his good points. The wrong he may do is only a small part of what he is, and it is a very poor expression of him. On the other hand, even the best person makes mistakes, forgets, can't even know enough or do enough to be considered "good." There is more bad in each of us than we have ever expressed. And there is more good in each of us than we have ever expressed. The hope of the happiness of mankind lies in the possibility that we may learn ways of developing more and more of the good in people.

When a baby is born, it isn't good or bad. It is ignorant and innocent. Only as it grows up and learns the differences between truth and falsehood, between helping and hurting, between giving and taking, between loving and hating, can it begin to do right and wrong. When it knows the difference, then it can make choices. Then it can have a conscience. It can act in ways that destroy and ways that build. It can do right and wrong.

A person's conscience may be weak or confused. It may be narrow and rigid. Or it may be a conscience that is sensitive and helps him judge life with wisdom. It may be like a red tail-light that throws a beam on what he has done. It may be like a headlight that shows him where he is going and what choices he has at a fork in the road.

WHAT IS A GOOD ACT AND GOOD CONDUCT?

For some people it is easy to live a good life; they seem to know just what to do. But most of us have to think about it. Nobody knows what is best every time he has to decide. Some people have trouble in knowing, most of the time.

One reason is that what makes sense and looks right now may not make sense and be right sometime later. Most of us want to do certain things today, without thinking about whether they are right or wrong, or what will happen later. If we want fun, we want it now.

If you have to decide what to do, you can ask yourself some questions:

1. Does this act or conduct make me respect myself more? Or less? Will it make me a better or a worse person?

2. Will this act help me do my job and fulfill my obligations? Or will it mean that I neglect or endanger them?

3. If the act brings me money or position or power or popularity, is it worth it? Does it endanger other, more important, things?

4. Will the people I respect the most approve or disapprove? Will the people who care most about me — my family and friends -think more or less of me? Will they understand this act?

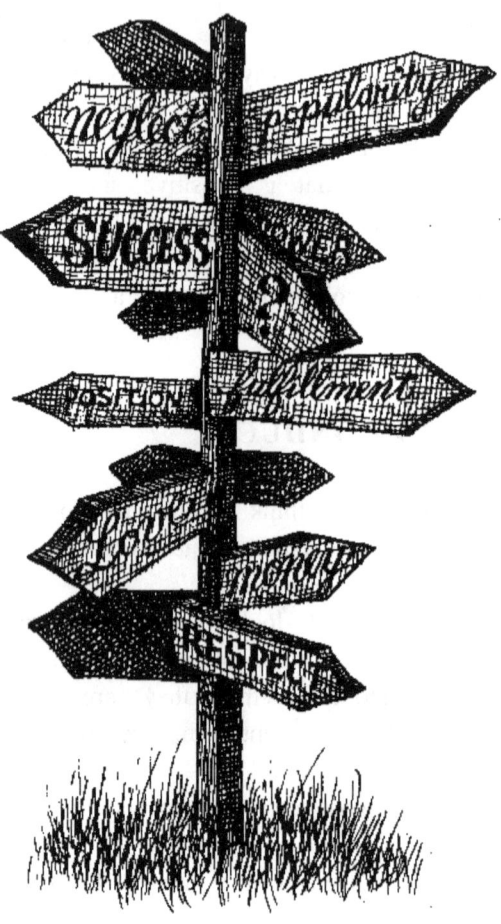

5. Would I approve it if my friend were to do it? Would I think more or less of him for doing it?

6. Suppose everybody were to do what I am doing. Would it be bad for me and other people?

7. If I have to make a difficult choice, which is the lesser of two evils?

Besides these questions there are a few others based on principles which you may find helpful in thinking out what to do, or how to judge conduct.

Is this behavior destructive? Will it hurt people? Or will it help?

Does it benefit only my people and people like me? Or will it benefit all kinds of people?

Does it exclude some people, or include all people? Does it make barriers and separate people, or does it bring about communication and understanding and unity?

Does it respect differences, or does it reject and crush differences?

Is the act good for me? Is it good for me at the expense of other people and the community? Is it good for others, but will it hurt me?

All of us are ruled by many feelings and desires and pressures. We would live much better and happier lives and be much wiser than we are now if we took more time to think over our actions and choices.

Anyone can benefit by talking problems over with someone else. Two heads are usually better than one. A close friend your own age can be a help. So can an older person whom you trust. Your favorite teacher or club leader or minister or priest or rabbi has a different experience and viewpoint from yours. And one of your parents may be of special help because of experience and because he or she knows you and cares about you. You don't have to follow the advice of any of these people. But you can be sure that after talking things out with them you will be much clearer about what you are deciding, and what it means in your life and the lives of other people.

WHAT LAWS DO ABOUT ETHICS

Through laws the community can agree to protect those things that it considers most important. The laws say what is forbidden, and what is required of people. In this way, life,, property, privacy, and reputation can be protected. Without a certain amount of trust and security and order, nobody would be safe in his home; no man would start a business, or be able to do much of anything. The businesses and farms and banks and government would all be at the mercy of the strongest and most ruthless individuals.

By defining crimes the community is saying that it is not up to the individual or his relatives and friends to claim injury, and retaliate and punish the offender. It is up to the government, the police, and the courts. The community says, "This damage which has been done to you is not just damage to you, but is damage to all of us." It guarantees to protect you and also prevents you from trying to take personal revenge and retaliation. In this way the community, through its laws, prevents quarrels and feuds which could hurt even more people and make more hate and violence.

The law is also important in settling disagreements where there is no crime.

Fair Play

When we are children we quarrel about toys, and argue about games. "The ball was in!" "The ball was out!" "I was first. You were second!" "No, *I* was first and *you* were second!" "That isn't fair!"

When we are older, there are differences and arguments, too.

A man may sign a contract promising to deliver goods or build a building. But maybe he doesn't do it. He may deliver bad goods. He may finish the building long after he promised he would.

Perhaps a scientist may discover a new drug or invent a new process, but another man may claim that he made the discovery or invention first.

Sometimes a writer reads a book and finds that someone has copied his ideas and words.

Two cars are in collision. Each driver blames the other.

Even though there is no crime, these disputes have to be settled.

The laws about contracts and patents and copyrights and damages were written to prevent injustice and to promote fair play. The courts try to help bring about fair play and prevent people from hurting each other.

If your property is damaged by someone or even by the government, you can sue in court. If you can prove damage, the party who caused it must pay you and make good the harm done.

But all the laws must have the moral support of the community. The people must feel that the laws are necessary and fair, and they must trust their officials to enforce them honestly. The judges who make the decisions must be impartial and they must try to get the facts. They must also use the wise decisions of the past as a guide. These past decisions are called "precedents." They are carefully kept in law books through all the years, so that there will be an accumulation of ethical wisdom for the guidance of future generations.

Guaranteeing Your Rights

There are other very important laws — perhaps the most important of all. They are part of the human struggle for a democratic way of life. They have come to us in various ways. Some have come through customs and court decisions made centuries ago. Some were born of bitter wars and bloody —revolutions. They have grown out of the struggle for religious freedom, for freedom of speech, for relief from injustice and oppression.

Our constitutional system assumes that every human being has certain rights that cannot be taken away by other citizens or by the government itself. We believe that these rights belong to us no matter what our religion or color or national, background, or whether we are rich or poor, educated or uneducated, male or female.

These "unalienable rights" do not depend on majority opinion. Even if everybody in the community dislikes you, you still are entitled to these rights. The American colonists felt so strongly about them that they refused to ratify the Constitution unless the amendments known as the Bill of Rights were assured of adoption.

The right to freedom of religion — to worship according to your beliefs or not to worship at all, in accordance with your conscience — is the first right guaranteed.

You have freedom to speak and print your thoughts. This freedom includes your right to meet with others to discuss and learn and teach, and to organize associations to protect and advance your ideas and interests.

You have the right to security of your person from arbitrary arrest and imprisonment, and you have the right to a fair trial.

You have the right to equal treatment whether in the matter of schooling or job opportunities or transportation or housing or recreation facilities or hospital care, no matter what your religion or color or national background.

Finally, you have the right to vote and take part in public affairs.

One of the most encouraging things for all those people who hope for a democratic and peaceful world is the growing interest in human rights. As each nation gains its independence and adopts a constitution for its own self-government, it adopts a bill of rights. In the United Nations, the Commission on Human Rights is one of the most important agencies trying to bring about agreement on an international Bill of Human Rights, guaranteed by all the nations. Someday this may be adopted and then anyone can appeal for justice to the World Court.

CAN LAWS MAKE PEOPLE DO WHAT IS RIGHT?

Laws can forbid acts that are wrong. Laws can help people be fair to each other. But laws cannot make people think or feel or do what is right.

It's like taking a horse to the water. You might lead him to the river or even pull him with a truck. But when you have him there, you cannot make him drink. And if he doesn't want to stand up, you cannot make him do so. He must want to.

Just so, you cannot force one person to like another person. You cannot make a person be generous. You cannot order a person to be kind or loving. These things grow out of his inner thoughts and feelings, and often depend on what kind of home and family he comes from.

Laws can *help* people be free. Laws cannot *make* people free. If people do not want to be free, if they prefer a dictator, if they do not know how to be free, no laws can help them.

And if people have no respect for one another, or if they do not believe in equal rights for all, no law can bring about fairness or justice among them.

Strong within each person must be the love of freedom and the strength to think and make choices and be responsible for his own actions.

The belief that all men have the same right to live, and the respect for all persons and for their rights and opportunities must be deep in the minds and hearts of the people. Each person must care about the rights of others as much as he cares about his own. Each person must really believe that he cannot have his own rights unless other persons also have theirs.

BIG ETHICAL ISSUES

We are living in an exciting and dangerous and wonderful time in human history.

It is an exciting time because it is a time of discovery. We are meeting new people and different people. We are exploring the inside of the atom, and the living cell. We are discovering new energies. We are reaching out into space and trying to find out whether there is life somewhere in the universe besides on our little planet.

It is a dangerous time because we have such knowledge and power that we can destroy each other and all life on this planet if we are not careful.

And it is a wonderful time because we now have the opportunity and the challenge to make life better than we ever dreamed before.

You are a citizen and a member of the community. Your voice and vote and behavior can affect the customs and laws and conditions under which we all live. Today no community exists by itself. No community can keep a narrow and rigid moral code. Trade, travel, new scientific inventions, education, and communication are helping people see that there are many ways of living and that life can be improved. The ideas of freedom and equality and peace are in the minds of more and more people. The dreams of a better life for all are a challenge to everybody who cares about the world. You can join with others to give strength to the things you believe in.

THREE CHALLENGES

Challenge 1. *How to get the people of the world to stop killing each other in wars, and make peace.*

In modern war, weapons are so dangerous that even those nations

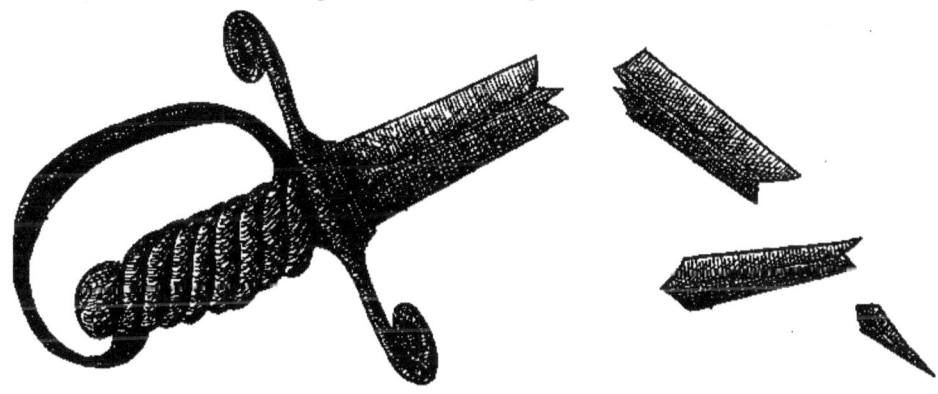

that could destroy other nations are afraid to use them. Nuclear bombs, fire bombs, bacteria bombs, and chemical weapons delivered by rockets and planes have put the whole human race in danger. A war between two nations may become a world war. And a world war would mean the use of these deadly weapons. So almost every sane and thinking person is concerned not only for his own nation and his own life, but also for the survival of the whole human race.

More and more people are trying to find ways of ending wars. Here are some of the ways:

Educating nations and people to respect each other.

Educating people to respect differences of religion and race, and differences of politics and cultural ways.

Increasing trade and travel and the exchange of ideas so that people will know each other better and see that they have things that other nations need and can use.

Making treaties about boundaries and disarmament.

Creating a strong United Nations so that nations can talk out their differences and work together when any of the nations seem to be in danger of going to war.

Creating such agencies as the World Court of International Justice to settle disputes, and the World Bank to lend nations money for preventing famine or plague or unemployment and for helping develop a better life.

Using foreign-aid programs to send food and medicines and machinery so that people can help themselves.

Sending international technical-assistance teams of farmers, engineers, water experts, doctors, teachers, and scientists to help deprived peoples.

Challenge 2. *How to get the people of the world to guarantee one another's freedom, and assure equal rights and opportunities for all.*

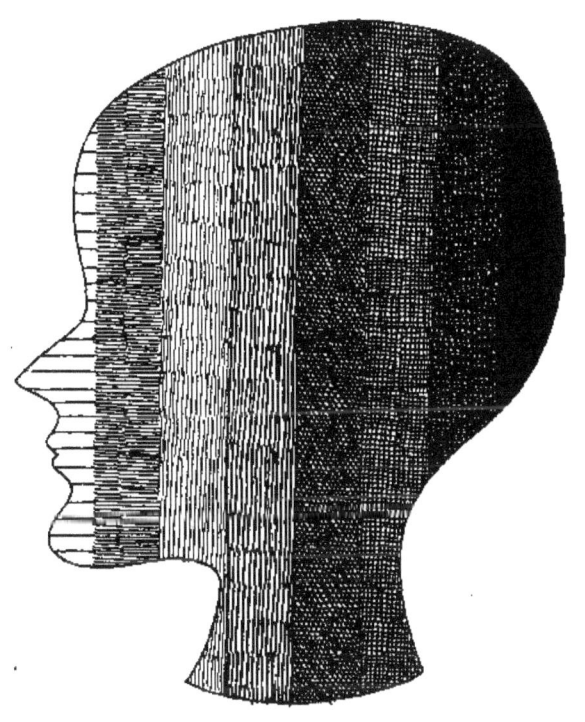

In almost every part of the world, people have had trouble living with others who are not like themselves. Differences of color or birth or language or religion have caused fear and distrust and even hate.

In the United States the population is made up almost entirely of people who came from other countries. Every group that has come has tried to find freedom and the opportunity to make a better life. But every group has learned that some people have been prejudiced against it.

Today the main problems of race relations are between "white people" and "colored people." Of course, this is an odd way of putting it, because we are all colored in different ways. There is no really white person. But by "colored" we mean mostly the brown and black people who are descended from those who came here from Africa, many of them as slaves. Even after slavery was abolished one hundred years ago, colored people were denied the schooling and jobs and fair trial and voting rights that were enjoyed by other Americans.

But now the ideas of freedom and equality and democracy for all men have been circulating in the world. All people are demanding equal status. The demand comes from the minority groups in our own country. It comes from people all over the world. Many people from the groups who have enjoyed their full rights are joining in the fight for equality for all.

A number of methods are being tried in the cause of racial equality. These are some of them:

Educating people who have been denied schooling, with special programs to help them.

Offering scholarships to help boys and girls who might not be able to afford to go on in high school and college, or to prepare for professions.

Setting up special training programs for specialized jobs.

Passing fair-practice laws to make for equal opportunity in jobs in government departments, industry, and trade unions.

Passing fair-practice laws to assure equal treatment in use of transportation, and eating and recreational places.

Passing fair-practice laws to assure equal opportunity to rent apartments and to rent and buy houses.

Setting up special programs to be sure that people know of their right to vote, and to help them register so that they can vote.

Establishing policies that will make sure that all people will get equal treatment in hospitals and clinics.

Establishing policies that will make certain that people of every race are treated the same in the Army, Navy, Marines, and Air Force.

Challenge 3. *How to arrange so that people can share the abundance of nature and of man-made productivity, to rid the world of poverty. How to get the benefits of automation with freedom and equality for all.*

Ours is a beautiful country. We are fortunate that we have fertile earth and varied climate and many rich natural resources. Our people have worked hard, and with the help of scientists and inventors and able business organizers have produced an abundance of all kinds of goods and services. Our farmers are efficient. Although only a small part of the population works on the farms, they have produced more food than we need for all the people of the United States — so much that we can sell food or give it away and store a surplus besides.

Many countries are not so fortunate. They lack our variety and rich natural resources. Many of them have suffered from famines and plagues and the destruction of wars. As a result, a few of their people are rich and some are well off, but the largest part of the population is very poor. Many people in Latin America and in countries like India and China lack food and medicine and decent housing and schools. Poverty is widespread — much more so than in the United States.

Because people who live in poverty have such a hard time bettering themselves and suffer so much sickness and hunger, they are often angry and desperate. They want to change things. Some want more democracy, with freedom and equality and popular rule. Some want the government to own and manage all the agriculture and industry and banking so that everybody will share more equally in the products of the economic effort.

Among the masses of those who have lived in poverty are many who hope that someday they will have a greater equality and a decent share of the products of the factories and farms. Some believe that a dictatorship of the workers is the only way. They do not believe that the present wealthy and powerful groups will share what they have or that they will permit democracy to be used by the people to make real changes for greater justice.

The groups who hold a belief in dictatorship are usually extreme and fanatical. They are against democracy and they fight each other.

We in America have had so much freedom and opportunity and faith in ourselves and in the future that we believe we can solve our problems without dictators. We have a strong faith in the democratic way of working out our problems.

Now we must face some new questions which will challenge our brains and wisdom. How can we use new inventions, and especially automation, without causing more unemployment and more poverty? This is a problem in the United States and in many other countries. It raises questions about how to train people for jobs and changing work. It raises questions about what our schools are for. It disturbs the values of property, for some things that people own will be worth more and some others will be worth less. Because of this, some people will want the changes, and others will fight them. But whatever we do to solve our problems, we must be sure to think about which is more important — property or people. And whatever we do, we must be careful to solve the problem of poverty. There are three big reasons why we should think about this.

First, we care about people and we want every man and woman and child in the world to be able to live and be free and healthy and happy. *Second,* we know that democracy is the best form of government and that people who suffer from poverty and ignorance and sickness have a hard time making democracy work. *Third,* we know that the world can never have peace so long as half of it has all the things it needs while the other half lives in poverty, and suffers and is unhappy.

HARD CHOICES

These three big ethical challenges are not easy ones. But they cannot be avoided. Nobody can escape them. Even your most personal desires and hopes can be ruined if there is war or racial strife or violent class conflict. These questions are challenges to your brains and to your wisdom. They give you a special opportunity to think out where you stand and what you intend to do as you grow older.

SOME WISE WORDS FROM THE PHILOSOPHERS

Best is the man who can himself advise;
He too is good who hearkens to the wise;
Who, himself being witless, will not heed
Another's wisdom, is worthless indeed.

Hesiod
(c. 720 B.C.)

Know thyself. The unexamined life is not worth living.

Socrates
(470-399 B.C.)

No one is born for himself alone. He owes himself in part to his country, in part to his parents, and in part to his friends.

PLATO
(427-347 B.C.)

Men should live by the rule of moderation. Extremes are bad. One should not be miserly or profligate. One should not be a coward, but also one should not be recklessly courageous.

ARISTOTLE
(384-322 B.C.)

Self-restraint and self-control and the mind in command of the body are the important rules of life. The duty of a citizen is not to consider his own interest distinct from that of others, as the hand or foot, if they possessed reason and understood the law of nature, would do and wish nothing that had not some relation to the rest of the body.

EPICTETUS
(c. a.d. 60)

Mankind is the embodiment of reason. Reason teaches man's duties.

MARCUS AURELIUS
(A.D. 121-180)

No man is an island, entire of itself; every man is a piece of the continent, a part of the main; if a clod be washed away by the sea, Europe is the less, as well as if a promontory were, as well as if a manor of thy friends or of thine own were. Any man's death diminishes me, because I am involved in mankind; and therefore never send to know for whom the bell tolls; it tolls for thee.

JOHN DONNE
(1573-1631)

Men who are governed by reason — that is, who seek what is useful to them in accordance with reason — desire for themselves nothing which they do not also desire for the rest of mankind, and consequently are just, faithful, and honorable in their conduct.

BENEDICT SPINOZA
(1632-1677)

It is easy in the world to live after the world's opinion; it is easy in solitude to live after our own; but the great man is he who in the midst of the crowd keeps with perfect sweetness the independence of solitude.

RALPH WALDO EMERSON
(1803-1882)

With malice toward none; with charity for all; with firmness in the right, as God gives us to see the right, let us strive on to finish the work we are in; to bind up the nation's wounds; to care for him who shall have borne the battle, and for his widow, and his orphan — to do all which may achieve and cherish a just and lasting peace among ourselves, and with all nations.

ABRAHAM LINCOLN
(1809-1865)

ETHICS IN THE STRUGGLE FOR DEMOCRACY

Pericles (c. 400 b.c.): **We are called a democracy, for the administration is in the hands of the many and not the few. . . . The law secures equal justice for all alike in private disputes.**

Magna Carta, 1215: **Of sixty-two articles enumerating the feudal rights of the barons, two went further:**
Number 39: **No freeman shall be taken, or imprisoned, or outlawed, or exiled, or in any way harmed, nor will we go upon or send upon him, save by the lawful judgment of his peers or by the law of the land.**
Number 40: **To none will we sell, to none deny or delay, right or justice.**

The Body of Liberties, 1641: **The code of laws adopted by the Massachusetts Bay Colony included the following articles:**
— **Equal justice under law for citizens and foreigners**
— **Freedom of speech and publication at any town meeting**
— **Right to jury trial**
— **Compensation for private property taken for public use**
— **Right of the people to elect those who will govern them**
— **Prohibition of slavery and of inhumane, barbarous, and cruel punishment**

The Declaration of Independence, 1776: **Adopted by the Continental Congress, this stated in part:**

We hold these truths to be self-evident, that all men are created equal, that they are endowed by their Creator with certain unalienable rights, that among these are Life, Liberty, and the pursuit of Happiness. That to secure these rights, Governments are instituted among Men, deriving their just powers from the consent of the governed.

The Declaration of the Rights of Man and the Citizen, 1789: **Adopted by the States General in France, this stated in part:**
— Men are born and remain free and equal in respect of rights
— Everyone is counted innocent until he has been convicted
— Every citizen may speak, write, and publish freely, provided he is responsible for the abuse of this liberty

The United States Bill of Rights, 1791: Adopted as the first ten amendments of the Constitution of the United States as a condition of its ratification, these state in part:

Number 1: Congress shall make no law respecting an establishment of religion, or prohibiting the free exercise thereof; or abridging the freedom of speech or of the press; or the right of the people peaceably to assemble and petition the Government for a redress of grievances.

Number 5: No person shall, be ... deprived of life, liberty, or property without due process of law. ...

The Universal Declaration of Human Rights, 1948: Adopted by the General Assembly of the United Nations, this states in part:
— All human beings are born free and equal in dignity and rights
— Everyone has the right to life, liberty, and security of person
— No one shall be subjected to torture or to cruel, inhuman, or degrading treatment or punishment
— No one shall be subjected to arbitrary arrest, detention, or exile
— The will of the people shall be the basis of the authority of government
— Everyone has the right to work, the right to rest, and the right to education

INDEX

Aristotle, 9, 61
Automation, 59

Babylonians, 13
"Bad" people, 44-45
Bill of Rights (United States), 51, 64
Blood price, 5
Body of Liberties, the, 62
Book of the Dead, 16
Borrowing, 30
Brown, John, 10

Capital punishment, 20
   arguments against, 20
   arguments for, 20
Challenges, ethical, 53-59
Choice, 1, 34, 45, 47, 52
Christianity, 14
Commandments, 13-14, 30, 33, 35, 38
   four important, 14
Commission on Human Rights (UN), 51
Conscience, 1, 11, 20, 45
Crime
   means of abolishing, 20
Customs, 5-8
   definition of, 6
   reasons for, 6-7
   reasons for changes in, 8
   tribal, 6

Declaration of Independence, 63
Declaration of the Rights of Man and the Citizen, 63
Defense, 17, 19
Democracy, 58, 59, 62-64
Dictatorship, 58
Donne, John, 61

Egyptians, ancient, 9, 13, 16, 37
Emerson, Ralph Waldo, 61
Epictetus, 61
Ethics
   definition of, 1
   derivation of word, 11
   purpose of, 1
   questions in, 2, 17, 19, 20, 25-26, 35, 36, 38, 39, 45-47
Ethos, 11

False witness, 26-29
Family, 31-33
   loyalty to, 31-33
Fear, 39
Feelings, personal, 39-40
Forgiveness, 42
Freedom, individual, 50-52, 54-56, 62-64
Freedom of speech, 51

Gandhi, Mahatma, 19
Golden Rule, 38
Good conduct, 45-47
   questions for judging, 45-47
"Good" people, 44-45
Gossip, 26
Greeks, ancient, 9, 11
Guilt, 39

Hall of Truth, 13
Hammurabi, 13, 35
Helping, ways of, 38-39
Hesiod, 60
Human beings, value of, 12-13, 17
Human rights, 50-52, 54-56, 62-64
Hurt, personal, 42-43
Hurting, ways of, 35-36

Individual, value of the, 12-13, 17
Isaiah (Old Testament), 38
Issues, ethical, 52-53

Jesus, 14, 19, 38
Judaism, 13-14
Jungle, law of the, 3

Killing, 15-20
   and capital punishment, 20
   and defense, 17, 19
   reasons for, 16
   and robbery, 19
   and self-defense, 17

Law of Righteousness, 37-38
Laws, 47-52
   and fair play, 48-49
   and individual rights, 50-52
Lies, 26
Lincoln, Abraham, 61

Lovejoy, Elijah, 10
Magna Carta, 62
Marcus Aurelius, 61
"Minus" ethics, 35-36
Moral code, 6-8, 14
    effect of, 7
    punishment for violating, 7
    reason for changes in, 8, 11
Moses, 13, 35

Name-calling, 28
New Testament, 38
Noah, 30-31
Nonviolence, 19

Parents, 30-34, 47
    loyalty to, 31
    need for, 31, 33
    obedience to, 33-34
    resentment against, 31
    respect for, 30-33
Pericles, 62
Philosophers, 11, 60-62
Philosophy
    meaning of word, 11
Plato, 9, 61
"Plus" ethics, 37-39
Poverty, abolishing, 57-59
Privacy, 28
Problems, talking over, 47
Promises, 29-30

Race relations, 55-56
Religion
    Babylonian, 13
    Egyptian, 13, 16
    freedom of, 51
Religions, world
    ethics and, 12-14
Reparation, 5

Reputation, 26
Retaliation, 3-5
Right and wrong
    judging of, 1
Rights, individual, 50-52, 54-56, 62-64
Romans, ancient, 9
Rules of life; *see* Customs
Rumor, 26

Secrets, 28
Self, attitude toward, 40-42
Self-defense, 17
Self-judgment, 40-41
Self-trust, 42
Slavery
    changing ethics of, 9-11
Socrates, 60
Soul, judging of, 13, 16
Spinoza, Benedict, 61
Stealing, 22-26
    definition of, 22
    reason for rules against, 24
    results of, 23-24
    ways of, 25

Ten Commandments, 13
Things
    importance of, 22
Torah, 37-38
Truth, concealing of, 27

Understanding, 42
United Nations, 51, 54, 64
Unity, need for, 3
Universal Declaration of Human Rights
    (United Nations), 64

War, abolishing of, 53-54
White lies, 29

"Zero" ethics, 36

www.ingramcontent.com/pod-product-compliance
Lightning Source LLC
Chambersburg PA
CBHW071746040426
42446CB00012B/2485